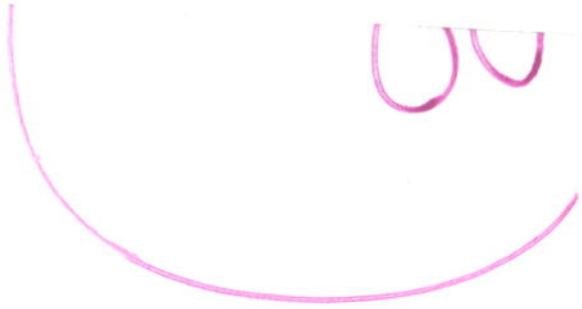

JUMP START Your Life

Choose your own lifestyle before someone chooses it for you.

Margot Larson

First edition published by:
Altern Publications
P.O. Box 206, Waterford, CT. 06385 USA

First Printing 2001

Printed in the United States of America

ISBN 0-9705021-0-9

Acknowledgement

I am grateful for the inspiration of the following philosophers, authors and all around wise people.

Wayne Dyer
Sarah Ban Breathnach
Abraham Maslow
Henry David Thoreau

Olga Fernandez, for her candid yet diplomatic editing skills.
My brother, Bob Mills, for his insight and his contribution to chapter 6.
Joy Taylor for designing the cover.
To my friends who read the first manuscript and encouraged me to continue.

This book is dedicated to

Monique

whose "love of life"
and courage inspires us all.

JUMP START Your Life

Choose your own lifestyle before someone chooses it for you.

Why wait for retirement to simplify your life?

What if you could choose your life style, NOW?

What are you waiting for?

Turn the page and learn why and how.

Contents

Welcome.

Let's set the tone for this journey.

Sit somewhere quiet and stare off into space or
close your eyes as you let your thoughts drift.

Remember your last really good vacation.
Recall the feelings of well being you experienced once you were totally unwound.

The mellowness,
The lack of urgency.
The feeling of calmness.
The flow, the ease.
A delightful sense of relaxation.

How would you like to rekindle and live that experience every week of your life?

Now, open your eyes, hold the thought and
learn how to make it a reality.

"This book is for people with dreams.
People who want to move on to a better lifestyle,
one that suits them."

Margot Larson

Preface

How to use this book.

I think it is important that you read this book very slowly. Take the time to think through and digest each step, each question. Approach it as a "work in progress" rather than a competition to finish it in record time.

Use it as your guidebook.

As you read, you will find that thoughts will surface. You will want to stop and ponder the questions and keep track of the answers that flow to you.

You don't have to read this in the order it is printed. You can skip forward to get clarification on a question that arises and may be covered in the pages ahead.

Don't be afraid to use a highlighter or pen and underline anything that inspires you or something you want to come back to later. You can even scribble in the margins and note spaces that have been provided for that purpose.

Consider getting a small notebook that you keep close at hand, whether at home, at your office, in your car, everywhere.

Let's talk a bit about the Where to work on this.

We all react to different stimuli and circumstances. So the following are examples of what has worked for some. You will eventually discover your most creative and thought provoking times and places.

If you like the ocean, then create the opportunity to sit on the beach, or on a bench listening to the surf. Take a ferry ride, a boat ride. Rent a cottage on the beach, a house at the top of a cliff for a weekend or a week. It doesn't have to be summer. Now that I live by the ocean, I find that I enjoy the spring and fall almost more than the summer. I don't have to share my space as much during those seasons. I can become so much more intimate with my thoughts. It's now "my" beach, with less noise and less distraction.

If you like the mountains, the woods, then do the same. Borrow someone's hideaway for a few days, off-season. Or make time for a long hike, or just sitting on a park bench in a beautiful spot.

At the beginning you may want to simply sit and think. Don't press too hard. Raise one or two questions. Then let your mind go blank. Listen to the sounds of the birds, the water. Smell nature. Be calm. Let yourself just float away. If you have worrisome or troublesome thoughts that surface, acknowledge them, and ask them to leave.

Don't expect to find all the answers on your first try. This process is intended to prepare you, to open up the windows and doors in order to allow freshness into your mind and heart.

If you are someone who already meditates, you have found your way to get to that sacred space in your head, in your heart.

The practice of quiet time and sacred space will help the answers to surface. Be patient. Practice will yield results. This leads to the great "*AHA! Moments.*" Make an effort to create that time and space. ***Dare to schedule it.*** Put it on your daily/weekly planner. Unless you plan for it, it will never appear on its own. It is a commitment, a promise to you – a promise you should not break. Why? Because truth, honor, ethics start with you. You must honor and respect yourself if you want others to do so. The source is within you.

You will begin to discover other more conventional spaces and times that give some reflective moments. In the shower, the daily walk or exercise, in the car, an airplane, lunch on your own, the library across from the office, waiting in the doctor's office, standing in a long line. You'll even begin to welcome delays and broken appointments that provide the gift of "found time." Assume that it was meant for you. Grab the opportunity. You might even be able to replace sleeplessness with some creative thinking.

Savor those moments just before you fall asleep and the first few minutes when you wake up. These are often the doors to communication with the inner you. Listen to the messages and thoughts that float to the surface. Write them down.

A friend said to me the other day, "It's hard to trust and have faith in the outcome. I don't remember ever getting a message, an inspiration or divine guidance on what to do in my life."

I advised her to learn to stay still, be open, stop moving all the time. She is like a bumblebee that never lands.

You have to wait for it to happen. It takes patience and practice. It will happen for you, too. An old Zen proverb to remember "When the student is ready, the teacher will appear."

1

Clarify and define your dream.

This process of clarifying and defining your dream will require some soul searching, some reflection, facing your truths and recognizing reality. You will want to put it all into perspective, to understand the "why" and "what" that you are seeking. Knowing this will help you make it a reality. Even when you find yourself taking some side trips while on the path.

Ask yourself a lot of questions. Write down the answers, without censuring or judgement as to whether or not it will work. Think of it as brainstorming. Later you will use this material to determine your path.

For instance,

- ***If money were not an issue, what would you do as your primary life endeavor?***

- ***What would give you the greatest sense of fulfillment in your lifetime?***

- ***What hobby, pastime, or cause is so meaningful that you wish you could spend a great deal of time doing it?***

If you find it difficult to identify what exactly you do want out of life, it may be easier to identify those things you definitely don't want in your ideal life. Perhaps, that is the best place for you to start.

- ***What type of circumstance or situation causes you the most stress at work?***

- ***Identify situations that cause you stress in your relationships.***

- ***Make a list of what you don't want in your life.***

Once you have done that, move on to exploring what you really would like. What is meaningful to you; what would bring you pleasure and peace. It is important to reach and focus on what represents the "good life", rather than simply running away from the bad. For example:

If you find yourself stressed and really hating your work situation because of a lousy relationship with a difficult boss or partner, this might lead you to believe that you could never work for an employer again and that you must leave the corporate world and start your own business. That's running away from what you don't want.

I know a lot of people who have taken this route for all the wrong reasons. The combination of their characteristics, strengths and needs does not lend itself to self-employment. In fact, to be successful they need the structure, direction and limited risk. That is certainly not the world of the entrepreneur.

To re-write the above scenario, what is needed is a compatible work environment, corporate culture and a boss or partner who values the talent and efforts of the individual, the employee. Striving for a better fit and defining a job that suits your lifestyle is better than simply running away from what you have. The danger of focusing too much on what you don't want could cause you to "jump from the frying pan into the fire." You are acting on the "rebound."

To help you determine what you really want out of life, here are few questions to ponder. You don't have to tackle them all at once.

1. ***Describe the type of environment, atmosphere in which you are the most comfortable.***

2. ***Do you feel that there is something in particular that has been missing from your life?***

3. ***What makes you the most proud of in your life, so far?***

4. ***What would you do if you were truly bold, if you were not afraid?***

5. ***On your 80th birthday, what would you like the testimonials to say? What would you like to be remembered for?***

6. ***If your life were a play, how would you like to write the ending? Write it down.***

____

____

____

____

____

____

The future belongs to those who believe in the beauty of their dreams.
- Eleanor Roosevelt

"I am the principle obstruction between where I am and where I want to be." (Author unknown)

Negative self-talk is an obstruction. For example, do you find that you criticize yourself, call yourself names, and discourage yourself in the course of daily living? Is that inner-voice a cheerleader or a critic? Become aware of the tone of your inner conversations over the next week.

Do away with negative self-talk. It does not serve a positive purpose. Reprogram it.

Here are two examples:
When a task goes astray or you make a mistake, how often do you lambaste yourself with, "What an idiot, I'm so stupid I can't get anything right?" Rewrite the script: "Oops! I guess that wasn't the best approach. I think I'll try something different next time and be more successful"

"I *shoulda* called the airport to check whether the flight was on time before driving all the way here. Now because of my stupidity, I have to wait another two hours." Rewrite: "In the future, I'll always call first before heading to the airport."

Since you can't rewind your life, go back in time and start over, why even go there? There is absolutely no value to "shoulda," "coulda," etc.

While on the topic of negative self-talk, when I conduct employment interviews, I can't begin to tell you how many times I have heard someone say to me: "You probably want someone younger to do this job, but I hope you you'll consider me anyway."

Rewrite:

"I bring a lot of experience and maturity that will undoubtedly make me a successful performer. I have a strong work ethic and a track record you can count on."

Do you see the difference? Break your old habits and change your language. It will improve the outcome and your self-esteem.

2

Identify your needs.

Part of being able to materialize your dreams, to plan and activate, is gaining an objective understanding of what your basic needs truly are.

Clarifying your dream isn't enough. You have to figure out how to attain your dream and be able to survive and thrive while living it. So what about money? Mortgage, car payment and college tuition are part of everyone's life. There is no way out of it, right? Is that a truth or consequence?

Let's take an objective look at the pressures driving your life and revisit your standards of living. You are probably living in a domino effect. The more you earn, the less you have.

What if you were to reinvent your life? Let's just play with that concept for a moment.

American society has convinced us that we must keep climbing up and earning more and more money each year; that we must have that four-bedroom house and that we must personally finance our child's $100,000 college degree. Do you know that there are many people in this country who have opted for an alternative lifestyle? One that we often envy. A lifestyle where they earn less and yet have the life they choose. They seem to be happier and don't appear to be needful.

NOTES

How did they do that? They got off that corporate career escalator and chose to live and work on the ground floor. They found a way to accomplish all they wanted, prioritized their needs and set about fulfilling their plan.

You can do it too, if that's what you choose. First, you must explore how you might be able to redesign your daily life and whether you could enjoy living it. We often go through life believing we have no choice in the matter. We accept the cards we have been dealt without questioning whether those cards were really meant for us. We must seek the courage and the wisdom to know that "giving something up is not necessarily doing without."

It is amazing how we barely make ends meet, it seems, even on two salaries. Then you lose your job, you make a few adjustments and it all works out very well to your utter surprise. It doesn't even hurt. I have experienced that twice in my life so far, as have thousands of others.

But you will never get to where you want to be, unless you are willing to reconsider the basics.

There is a story about a woman who, upon entering a large vacant apartment that she was to appraise, heard the door lock behind her. She ran back to the door, pushing, kicking, and propelling her body against it in a desperate effort to get out. She was so distraught at being locked up and feeling trapped, that she never took a close look around or ventured around the corner, or looked behind the drapes. She did not see the two French doors (unlocked) at the other side of the room nor did she consider the two large windows. She focused on the closed door and did not investigate further.

In your life, every room has at least one door, sometimes there are two. Go find all the doors. Then, you can choose where to enter and where to exit.

NOTES

Let us differentiate between "Cost of Living" and "Standard of Living."

Cost of Living is the actual cost for your basic needs: housing, food, transportation, and health. It's the car that will get you there. No frills, no options. The basic black dress.

Standard of Living is a choice of how you live: the accessories, the luxuries. In a car, it's the sunroof, the leather package, the high performance (V-6 or V8) and special tires. With attire, it's the jewelry, the scarf, the matching pocketbook and shoes.

Too often, we make assumptions such as, "I can't leave this job I hate because I would not have money to pay the mortgage and health insurance." We make the assumption without first examining the issue in specific terms. How many months could you manage without a job? Would you need to pay the health insurance right away? Would you be eligible for unemployment insurance? Could you take a temp or part-time job while job searching for a "career" opportunity? Could you work with a Consumer's Credit Council to freeze your mortgage payments and other debt temporarily while unemployed? If you got very desperate, could you sell something, downsize, borrow from family or friends? What is the worst-case scenario? What is the best-case scenario?

Abraham Maslow describes our basic needs as:

1. Physiological Needs – Oxygen, food, water, shelter.
2. Safety.
3. Love, Affection and a Sense of belonging
4. Self-Esteem and respect.
5. Self-actualization. * (Refer to Chapter 7 for definition)

I have observed an interesting cycle among my peer group.

We get trapped into high-powered or demanding careers or jobs because we believe we have to, in order to support our lifestyle and its financial commitments.

Sometimes we are the victims of "golden handcuffs." The compensation and benefits are so good we don't have the courage to give it all up.

As a result of the high level of stress, we sometimes reward ourselves with multiple and/or expensive hobbies and/or vacations each year. We justify it on the basis of "mental health" to cope with the amount of stress in our lives.

Now here's a thought: What if we changed the job/career and eliminated the stress. Then we might not feel compelled to have to take the expensive vacation. This reduces the need to make "enough" money to afford the exotic vacation.

And so, we break the cycle.

Let me share an example of a friend who was in an employment situation that appeared to be verbally abusive. She put up with harassment from her supervisor. She did not like it, but she kept taking it because she felt she had no choice. She had to work. She was thinking of it in terms of all or nothing.

She was under a great deal of stress and her health was suffering. Her kidneys were shutting down, her heartbeat was affected, and she suffered migraine headaches and more. And yet, she wasn't willing to leave.

Several of us pressed her to make a decision. We showed her the choices she had and helped her prioritize.

I asked her how she would advise a client who was the victim of domestic abuse over and over again. She quickly responded, "I would tell her to get out of that situation and take control of her life." I suggested she take her own advice. She was leaving for a Florida vacation in a few days and was considering giving her notice upon her return.

Two days later, I spotted an advertisement in the Sunday newspaper for a job that sounded just right for her. At my urging, she pursued the opportunity the next day and was invited to an interview immediately. The following week, the employer called her in Florida and offered her the job, not at the going rate they had quoted her but at five thousand dollars higher than she expected.

For two years she put up with an impossible situation, making herself ill believing she could not leave her job because she might not find another. While she talked about her plight, she was not taking action to improve the situation. She was paralyzed by her doubts and fears and thinking one-dimensionally. Once she mobilized, she got a better job at a higher wage and made a seamless transition.

Her mind was closed to the opportunities that were in front of her all the while. Just like the woman in the previous story, she made assumptions without exploring her basic needs. Do you sometimes find yourself exhibiting similar behavior?

If you are having trouble visualizing how it might be possible to do with less, to make a major life style change, go talk to people who have accomplished it. They will be delighted to tell you how they did it. Don't take my word for it, do your research.

There are a lot of success stories and books written, such as *"Do what you love and the money will follow."* The skeptics will say "Sure. Sounds good but it wouldn't work for me." And I say, "What if it could? Think about that for a while."

"I learned this, at least, by my experiment: That if one advances confidently in the direction of his dreams, and endeavors to live the life which he has imagined, he will meet with a success unexpected in common hours." **Henry David Thoreau**

NOTES

Here's another perspective. One day, an expert in time management was speaking to a group of business students and, to drive home a point, used an illustration those students will never forget. As he stood in front of the group of high-powered overachievers he said, "Okay, time for a quiz."

He pulled out a one gallon, wide-mouthed Mason jar and set it on the table in front of him. Then he produced about a dozen fist-sized rocks and carefully placed them, one at a time, into the jar. When the jar was filled to the top and no more rocks would fit inside, he asked, "Is this jar full?" Everyone in the class answered "Yes."

Then he said, "Really?" He reached under the table and pulled out a bucket of gravel. Then he dumped some gravel in and shook the jar causing pieces of gravel to work themselves down in the space between the big rocks.

Then he asked the group, once more, "Is the jar full?" By this time the class was on to him. "Probably not," one of them answered. "Good!" he replied.

He reached under the table and brought out a bucket of sand. He started dumping the sand in the jar and it went into all the spaces left between the rocks and the gravel. Once more he asked the question, "Is this jar full?"

"No!" the class shouted. Once again he said, "Good."

Then he grabbed a pitcher of water and began to pour it in until the jar was filled to the brim. Then he looked at the class and asked, "What is the point of this illustration"? One eager beaver raised his hand and said: "The point is, no matter how full your schedule is, if you try really hard, you can always fit some more things in it!" "No," the teacher replied, "that is not the point."

"The truth this illustration teaches us is: ***"If you don't put the big rocks in first, you will never get them in at all. "***

What are the big rocks in your life? Your children? Your loved ones? Your education? Your dreams? A worthy cause?

So tonight, or in the morning, when you are reflecting on this short story, ask yourself this question, "What are the *big rocks* in my life?" Make a list of them.

Then remember to put these BIG ROCKS in the jar first or you'll never get them in at all. If you sweat the little stuff (the gravel, the sand), then you'll fill your life with little things you worry about that don't really matter, and you'll never have the real quality time you need to spend on the big important stuff.

You may feel clear about the needs you have just identified, but confused about how it will relate to the reality of life, the finances. Finances help fuel the dream, the priorities. You can't ignore that. That will be covered in Chapter 6. (If you don't want to wait, go ahead and skip forward to it now.)

3

Get started.

"If not you, Who? If not now, When?"
– Abraham Maslow

Are you ready to begin exploring and to mobilize into action? If the answer is NO, what is standing in your way? What will it take for you to be ready? What is the right set of conditions that will inspire you to take the first step? Write down your answers.

What are your fears? List the fears and doubts that create obstacles in your life. Have they grown with you since childhood? Stare at them objectively. Sometimes when you recognize and understand their source, they begin to lose their power over you. What is the worst that would happen if you looked at them straight on and then blew them away? I have often found that when I verbalize them and hear them out loud, I suddenly understand how that fear came to be and it no longer applies. By recognizing it consciously, I can move past it.

Hidden fears and doubts will come back to sabotage your efforts if you don't bring them to consciousness.

NOTES

Take them out of your subconscious and put them on paper. Then take pleasure in tearing them up, burning them, whatever suits your fancy. Do away with them.

Having reached this point, you can now recognize the obstacles and be aware of when they make you hesitate and procrastinate. Once you become aware of your self-manipulation, you can begin to rewrite how you will move through life.

Why not start NOW, as opposed to tomorrow ?
You will be pleased with yourself when you do.

How many of us have watched our parents – save the good linen, save all their money, wait to take that precious trip until it was too late. One of them got sick or died.

Stop making excuses why today isn't good. Don't keep mulling it over trying to justify about the best time.

Just do it!

Begin by listing one small step you could do today. What could you commit to do once a week? What would you like to accomplish within the next month? Be realistic. Don't plan for more than you can handle in a short period of time. The important thing is to start and keep moving forward.

One Christmas, my young nephew, Jim, gave us all a "Round Tuit." It was a colorful cardboard circle with the words "Round Tuit" inscribed on it. His attached note read something like this:

"Remember that project you wanted to undertake, that trip you wanted to plan, that letter you wanted to write when you got around to it. Now at last you have your own personal "round tuit" that will allow you to get it all done. Use it wisely."

You, too, can enjoy the same gift. It's located in the back of this book.

I also remember a conversation with my Uncle George. George and Rose lived in a very small apartment in an urban setting. They did not travel much. They lived very frugally on limited retirement funds. At 80 years old, Rose was still full of life, interests and youth. My uncle was more sedentary.

As they contemplated the coming of winter, I suggested they take a trip to Florida to visit my mother, who lived alone and craved company. The idea sounded good to me because it would resolve two situations. It would give my mother company and it would provide them with a sunny vacation at a very low cost.

My uncle's quick response was, "Been to Florida once. Why go again?" That mindset left me speechless. Not even my enthusiasm or zest could make a difference to overcome that rationale and closed mind.

What's your first response to life? Do you immediately see why something won't work, or do you look for the creative ways to make something work? With repeated practice, the mind can be taught to seek the positive solutions to any situation.

NOTES

Let's talk about the present.

Are your present circumstances so enjoyable that it entices you to stay there? Then, I ask, Why are you reading this book? This book is for people with dreams. People who want to move on to a better lifestyle, one that suits them.

About the past.

There are a lot of people who live in and through the past. Don't get me wrong. I am not opposed to history and good memories. However, when all the stories in your life, all the examples you use, all the people you talk about come from a period of time more than 10 years ago, it implies that your past is all you have. You are neglecting "the present" and you obviously doubt the potential of your future. If this sounds like you, and you are less than 70 years of age, you are wasting valuable time and energy.

On the other hand, if you are over 80 years old, reliving your memories may have been part of the Master Plan. Spend the earlier decades of your life building memories and when aging seriously restricts your activities, you can be sustained and stimulated by recounting these wonderful memories.

However, if you start reliving your memories at 42, you and your friends will be long bored with your stories by the time you reach 60.

***"Do not be afraid that your life will end.
Be afraid that it will never begin." Author unknown***

About the future.

Here is one last impetus to get you going. What if you learned tomorrow that you had a terminal disease or a life-threatening condition and had only five months to live?

And what if during those five months, you would be blessed with feeling reasonably well and could be active? How would you change your life?

What are the three things you would want to do?

What would you want to take care of while you still can?

Reflect and write any other perspective that comes to mind.

So you say: "Wait a minute. I don't have cancer."

The example of a disease gives you a time frame to work within. The end can as easily come from a car accident, plane crash, tornado, avalanche, whatever, in which case you would not have advance notice.

Why not consider this to be your advance notice; *your* **WAKE UP CALL** *to propel you forward.*

NOTES

4

Move forward.

Take baby steps. Don't expect to get it all done in one session. This will take questioning, reflection, determination and time.

This is a process, a journey of your life.

Perhaps, in some rare cases, some of you may go off to the mountains, the seaside, on a personal retreat and will turn this process into a marathon session, if that is what works best for you.

Others will start this process and it will be ongoing over several months and perhaps a few years. You will find that the more you pursue your thoughts, dig deeper, scrutinize your answers, you may revise and refine your plans, your goals. It's OK. Consider it an evolution. Recognize the importance is that you start, continue and see progress and results.

Make the time rather than expecting to find the time. Write it on your calendar; schedule an appointment with yourself. Treat that appointment as you would a very important client. One you would not cancel without a critical reason. Keeping this appointment with yourself will make you a better and more successful person in the long run. Isn't that reason enough to change?

It's your life. Who's in charge?
If it isn't you, then who?

NOTES

Learn to write down your questions and your reflections. What do you want to accomplish? What steps could you take to get there? Make a plan.

Be sure that each step is very small so that the process does not overwhelm you.

Example: Say you decided you want to write a play or build a futuristic energy efficient house. If your action plan starts with "Conduct Market Research." I will bet that it will take a long time to get to and through that action step. Instead, develop an action plan that reads more like this:

1. Spend one hour a week checking Internet sources and the library as to what already exists on this topic.
2. Identify potential competition.
3. Determine who to contact, to interview to gather information.
4. Prepare a list of questions.
5. Initiate one contact per week.
6. Keep notes of these interviews.
7. Find out who has been successful in this field and why.
8. Find out who has failed and why.

Get it? Don't be discouraged if your progress seems to be steering you in a slightly different direction. It's a journey, an adventure. Be curious as to where it will lead.

Your next steps:

Be sure to celebrate small victories. Train yourself to focus on your success. The best way to focus on success is to recognize what you have accomplished so far. Don't let a day or a weekend go by without listing at least one success. This will give you the self-confidence and stimulation to continue movi ng forward. If you find it difficult to practice this, get a friend or family member to commit to do it with you.

As an entrepreneur, I have created Success Teams for that purpose. We meet specifically to review and share our successes. We use each other as a sounding board for new ideas and obstacles. Perhaps you will want to create a Success Team with two or three others committed to helping each other blossom.

5

Monitor your mindset.

Whenever you drive though some impoverished parts of the country, do you ever wonder how it is that two people can be born in the same situation, and one goes on to become a great success while the other remains in that same environment and simply exists without growth, fulfillment and happiness?

Take siblings, for instance – same parents, same environment, same obstacles, same opportunities, same education and totally different outcomes. Some may say it is genetic. I say it is mindset. It is what you believe.

My favorite philosopher, author and great teacher, Dr. Wayne Dyer, in his many presentations, relates a metaphor of two babies in their mother's womb, whom he calls Ego and Spirit. *(This is an excerpt that has been paraphrased.)*

Spirit says to Ego, "I know you are going to find this difficult to accept, but I truly believe there is life after birth." Ego responds, "Don't be ridiculous. Look around you. This is all there is. Why must you always be thinking about something beyond reality? Accept your lot in life."

A while later, Spirit adds. " Ego, I also believe that there is a Mother." Ego responds, "How can you be so absurd? You've never seen a Mother. The idea of a Mother is crazy. This is your reality."

One more time Spirit attempts to share her beliefs. "Ego, please listen without rejecting my idea. Somehow, I think that all the pressures we feel, the uncomfortable movements and continual repositioning is getting us ready for a place of glowing light and we will experience it very soon. And along with that light, when we experience it, we are going to meet Mother face-to-face and know an ecstasy that is beyond anything we have ever experienced up until now." Ego replies, "Now I know you are absolutely insane. There is no Mother. There is no light. Spirit, this is our reality. Learn to face it."

One of the many lessons to be derived from this story is that, often some of us *know*, sense the opportunity, have faith in an outcome that we have no evidence to support. And yet we must trust and believe in that "knowing." Just because someone else claims that our beliefs are crazy and insane does not make us wrong. That's only their opinion. Listen to your "Spirit", not the messages of your negative "Ego." You must first believe and feel it before you can manifest the dream.

Throughout this process, know that you will encounter the skeptics. In the beginning, as you start to dream and redesign your life, you may not want to share this with many people because nothing deflates us quicker than being around skeptics and negative thinkers. Once confidence is gained in this new process – share this with people in your life, as you feel appropriate or helpful to you or to them. This is a process of learning to be self-responsible.

Remember: We are talking about "choosing your own lifestyle before someone chooses it for you." What you want in your life may not be what everyone else wants for you.

It is important to recognize and know the following principle of life: ***What you think about expands.*** If you think about your success, you will get more of it. Whenever you think that you can't do it, you are right. You probably can't, because your mindset is self-limiting. You will usually live up to your expectations.

We are programmed by the messages we hear as children. In order to move forward, we must reprogram these messages. Negative self-talk and childhood baggage is as damaging to your life today as introducing a brand-new computer software program right out of the box and it is loaded with viruses.

Know that you can do anything that you set your mind to.

Here's an example. My friend Steve was in a car accident many years ago when his little sports car attempted to climb a tree. His elbow was severely damaged when it went through the window. After surgeries, he was told that he might be able to regain perhaps 10-20% of its use, but that would be the max. He did not accept the prognosis, and decided to prove the doctor wrong. He did it. Through hard work and determination, he recovered probably 80% use of that elbow. Steve opted not to accept someone else's perspective and instead created his own.

You may recall that until Frank Short broke the speed record for running a 4-minute mile, no one considered that it could be done. Everyone aspiring to match the standing record of a 6-minute mile had been told that beating it could not be done simply because no one had ever done it. Most accepted that premise. Except, of course, Frank Short.

Remember the saying: "*You have to see it to believe it.*" Rewrite that one: It should read: "*You have to believe it in order to see it happen.*"

You have the power to attract into your life that which you want. So, why not attract good stuff instead of bad luck? Make your own luck. Dwell on abundance rather than scarcity.

Why is it that some people see a glass half-full while others see it half-empty? Do you know that it takes less energy to be positive than it does to be negative? I think negative people don't accomplish much.

So try the positive, optimistic approach – it might work. Ah! What a pleasant surprise that might be! What do you have to lose?

When I was in my late teens, I was rather morose, lot of extremes, feeling very high one moment and then, very low the next. One day I observed how people were always attracted to certain jovial individuals. So I decided to try it. I decided to fake happiness. Guess what? It worked. It drew people to me, I felt less lonely and next thing I knew I even believed I was a happy person.

Why is it that we so often feel guilty about having a good time, or enjoying ourselves? Some of us have the impression that if it feels good, it must be bad. Also, some of us feel guilty if we are not productive all the time. There's a feeling that quiet time, doing nothing, means we are lazy. These are two of the old programs from childhood that have infiltrated our personal and professional lives.

I bet that unless you are really high up on the corporate ladder, chances are you would never take the time in your workday to openly read a business magazine or simply stare into space and reflect or analyze a situation. Why, someone might think you are "goofing" off!

This is very interesting behavior from a world that is no longer industrial but rather deals in intellectual capital and services to customers. It is not as though we are falling asleep at a machine. Our jobs are not manual. They are intellectual. So how is it that openly utilizing your intellect feels wrong?

We live in a society where not taking a vacation in three years is perceived as an achievement, something to boast about in the corporate boardroom. How pitiful!

We are very careful to be sure that the captain of our airplane or the engineer of our train is not over tired and so we limit the number of continuous hours they are allowed to work in a month. This is done for safety reasons. It's common sense. It implies that critical thinking might be diminished when over extended.

So how is it that we don't seem to apply this same criteria to the leaders of billion dollar corporations, to ER doctors and surgeons, the designers and fabricators of critical parts for moving vehicles and airplanes, or the engineer working on a nuclear reactor or to ourselves?

What a strange society we are. I guess this is what is known as an oxymoron. Sounds more like a derivative of "maxi-moron."

Accomplishments and success are born in the heart and in the mind. They are not just the result of money and opportunity.

NOTES

6

Take charge of your financial fate.

The key to financial success lies in controlling your expenses. Most people think that the solution is to earn more money.

If your income is $3,000 a month and you are having trouble making ends meet, you will have even more trouble at $5,000 a month and be totally out of control at $10,000 a month. You need to determine where you are currently spending your money, and then establish a budget.

A budget is nothing more than setting priorities. Your first priority should be your **savings**. This principle is sometimes called "pay yourself first." To determine how much you want to save you will find recommendations in the section on **Planning your Retirement** below.

First, establish where you are now spending your money, by regrouping all your outlays into main categories, such as:

- **Housing.** The cost of your residence (taxes, repairs & maintenance, insurance, etc).
- **Household**. The cost of operating the **household** (food, furniture, appliances, hygiene, cleaning, energy for heat, air conditioning & lighting, etc).
- **Clothing** and accessories for all members of the family.

- **Communications** (phone, cable TV, Internet, cell phone, newspaper & magazine subscriptions).

- **Transportation** (all automobile expenses, commuting costs, etc).

- **Education** (courses, self-improvement books & tapes, subscriptions to business & professional periodicals, memberships, etc).

- **Medical** (includes the cost of medical insurance, of dental & eye care, prescription and non-prescription drugs, etc).

- **Travel & entertainment** (vacations, restaurant dinners, theatre outings, membership & subscriptions to travel & entertainment-related groups or publications, magazines & book purchases).

- **Personal.** Use this category for cash you carry for incidentals. This helps avoid the need to account for every dollar you spend, for example, you may allocate $100 per week for small payment you make in cash). Also use it for items not elsewhere classified such as gifts and donations (you might put term life insurance here while you put whole life in the savings category).

- **Savings** (include money put aside for retirement, for major projects, whole life insurance etc)

It is not important where you classify your items of spending or what you call your categories. Just be consistent in your classifications, which are tools to identify where your money goes and where you want it to go. Some find it practical to list the same categories that would be used for income tax reporting.

I have included some worksheets that might be helpful. You will find them at the end of this chapter. Once you have completed your categorization and added up the total you are spending in each category on a monthly and annual basis, the total of all categories will most likely exceed your income.

Next, go through each category and decide which expenses can be eliminated or reduced to attain a balanced budget. You will instinctively know which items are more important to you and which are expendable. It is a little like cleaning out your clothes closet. Once you have balanced your current situation you can move on to look for ways to increase your income.

There are no shortage of books and tapes available to help you with this. Some experts say that you should reinvest 10% of your income on self-development, which includes developing your skills to increase your earnings.

Be sure to focus your energies where you will get the greatest return and delegate or outsource those areas that aren't your bailiwick.

Planning for Retirement

Whether you are 25 years old, 35, 45 or 55, it is important to stop and plan for your retirement. Your first step is to take stock. Establish what you own, what you owe, add what you earn and what you spend. Now think about the lifestyle you would like for your retirement. Once you are fairly clear on this, I strongly recommend making an appointment with an independent financial consultant for the purpose of finding out how much you need to save to attain your retirement goals.

Sure this will cost you a few hundred dollars. However, this is an investment that can mean hundreds of thousands by the time you retire. With information on your present assets, liabilities, earnings and savings a good independent financial planner will be able to use software at his disposal to make projections and arrive at recommendations for a savings plan,

He or she will need some additional input from you to determine your risk tolerance, your feelings about the future, etc., which are needed to chose an average inflation rate and an average rate of return on your savings, your potential for increased employment income, etc.

Once you have set out on a path with the help of the planner, you can probably continue on your own with a periodic review with the planner (I suggest once a year) to monitor your progress and to ensure that you remain on the right track.

If you have not done so before, you may want to take the time to itemize your assets and your liabilities and get a look at the big picture.

Wen I did that exercise many years ago, it became clear to me to pay off my debt with high interest rates rather than earning 4% on savings. It also incited us to consolidate our assets, liquidate properties that carried debt, responsibility and frustrations, thereby simplifying our financial management. This plan worked in our favor when we found our income suddenly dry up because of changes in our circumstances.

Worksheet

Monthly output

Housing: mortgage or rent, R.E. taxes,
major repairs, maintenance, insurance. __________

Household: food, furniture, cleaning, and utilities. __________

Clothing: hygiene, cosmetics, and personal care
(haircuts, massage). __________

Communication: telephone, cable, TV,
Internet, newspaper, magazine. __________

Transportation: car insurance, taxes,
auto expense, parking, commuting cost. __________

Education: courses, self-improvement
books and tapes, membership dues. __________

Health Care: medical insurance, medical care
(i.e. dental, vision, prescription, chiropractic,
physical therapy and gym). __________

Personal: This category for pocket cash expenditures. __________

Miscellaneous: Other insurance premiums.
Hobbies, boat costs, club memberships, etc. __________
*Note: interest on loans, charge cards, late fees
classified under specific category of purchases.*

Savings: __________
Total Outgoing: __________

MONTHLY INCOME: ______________

Now, go back and figure out how can you reduce all the outputs in order to increase the savings.

NOTES

WORKSHEET 2

If you have never done this exercise, you may find this helpful and enlightening.

Assets	**Value**
Real Estate	________
Automobiles	________
Boats	________
Stock/Funds Investments	________
Retirement Plans	________
Life insurance cash value	________
Savings	________
Total Assets	________

Liabilities	**Value**
Mortgage	________
Loans	________
Alimony, child support, Court judgement	________
Total Liabilities	________

NOTES

7

Break away from the "tribe."

If you want to better yourself, you must do something different than others are doing, and probably different than what you are doing right now. If you don't rethink and apply a new approach in the future, you will continue to get the same results you have in the past.

You must be willing to live without the approval of those around you and not be unduly influenced by the opinion of others. It is time to differentiate between needing and wanting the approval of others in order to move forward.

The "tribe" will tell you it can't be done. That's their role. They want you to do it "their" way. Who is the "tribe?" The "tribe" is the famous "**they** as in "you know what they say." "They say it's best to…." " They say you can't!"

When I opted not to return to corporate employment and instead do contract work as it comes along, my former co-workers felt sorry for me. A lot of people, even after five years of running my own business, still kept asking me whether I had found a job yet. I remember telling a former co-worker once how I had just turned down a top job with a major publishing company and how excited I was with my decision. She looked at me as though I had lost my marbles. She felt totally perplexed by my behavior.

I remember discovering, at one point of my life, that while on one hand I would describe myself as an individualistic, somewhat non-conformist, out-of-the-box thinker (which also corresponded to how my friends and colleagues would describe me), that there was something inside me that still cared what others thought of me. I thought I needed validation. I realized upon reflection that it all stemmed from early messages and programming, "…but what will others think? What will the neighbors say? I have finally progressed to responding out loud: "So what? Who cares?" In order to move beyond that limiting belief.

Perhaps you will want to re-examine your attachment to the "tribe." Sometimes it is helpful to play out your worst fears. What is the worst that will happen if your mother doesn't approve of your decision? Who are you trying to impress? What is causing you to second-guess yourself? Are **you** satisfied with the outcome, even if others might not be? What is that telling you?

Take the time to reflect and recognize whom you truly admire in this world, either now or someone from the past. Why? What is it about them that stimulates your interest and your respect? Are these attributes that you would like to embrace, to emulate?

Abraham Maslow describes a **"self-actualized person"** (a person having achieved greater awareness) as follows:

- **Someone who is independent of the good opinion of others**. *While we all enjoy the approval of others, we should be able to exist without it. The approval or opinion of others should not govern our lives or our actions.*

- **Someone who does not get off on having power over others.** *That is, someone who doesn't always have to be right. Some people seem unable to comprehend that they don't have to make someone else wrong in order to feel right.*

- **Someone who is not attached to the outcome.** *This means that you do the best you can, but if the outcome is not as desired, it is not devastating. In other words: If you can't change the outcome, change your perspective.*

A self actualized person is not a burden to society or to those around them.

If you want to achieve personal growth, you must step out of your comfort zone, at least once in a while.

Becoming a self-actualized individual is indeed a goal to strive for, and one that might take an entire lifetime to master consistently. This should not, however, deter us from practicing.

NOTES

8

Create momentum and monitor your progress.

One of the most common mistakes we all make is worrying and focusing on what is undone, what we must do, and not spending enough time identifying and recognizing our successes and praise ourselves for what we have done so far.

I have a habit of going past my mark without noticing. I get frustrated and whine about not having yet achieved something and when I take the time to check, I realize that I have already met my goal and have actually gone beyond it. My lesson is to keep monitoring my progress so that I will know when I reach it. A friend once told me that I am so focused on the goal, that I don't always take the time to notice and enjoy the journey. Shame on me.

At the end of each day, take the time to count your accomplishments, and recognize how far along you have come, no matter how small the steps are. This should be done before moving forward. You will feel much better about yourself.

List that day's accomplishments and/or successes in your daily planner, your journal or notebook. Pat yourself on the back.

Let me repeat this very important premise: When you focus on success, you'll get more of it. When you focus on failure, obstacles and oversights, you will get more of them, too.

NOTES

Once you have noted your progress, then you can face the next steps with greater energy and confidence. It is much easier to look at the last half of the list rather than the whole list. It is like climbing a ladder or a mountain. Focus on the present and the future will take care of itself.

Developing a habit, I have been told, takes 21 consecutive days of doing it. Practice discipline rather than procrastination.

If you find that you have slipped back into an old undesired habit, it's OK.. Don't let it get you down. Just catch yourself and immediately return to the new you.

Any progress forward, any step completed, no matter how small, is success.

It is critical to recognize and reward success daily, weekly, annually. Take a few moments at the end of each day or week and list what you have accomplished. This is particularly important on a difficult and bad day. You will feel much better about yourself.

Encourage yourself. Cheer yourself on. It's really OK to do so regardless of what you were programmed to think as a child.

Some of us have picked up some very bad personal habits from strict, but well-meaning parents, teachers, the rabbi, the nuns, etc... Let's move beyond that stage, after all, we are no longer 15. It's time to own up to our own behavior, reactions, feelings and thoughts. Let's accept accountability for who we are.

Identify one or two people who can be good cheerleaders for you. Stay away from the "Naysayers."

One of the ironies of life is that when we are under the most stress, we often stop our exercise or meditation or relaxation techniques because we are too busy. We avoid calling friends, mentors because we are feeling down. Isn't that absurd? That's when we need them most.

It is the same with your plan. Reach out for others when you are in a slump. Don't hibernate. Ask, and accept help. (This may be a new practice or even a stretch for you.) Remember, it's for a good cause – YOU.

Give your action plan to a trusted friend and ask them to check on your progress. This really works for me because I am highly accountable and I would not want them to ask me if I had done what I planned to do and have to answer no.

9

Adapt and thrive in your new lifestyle.

OK, so now you've "got a life." What do you do with it? There is an old expression that is very telling: ***"Be careful what you wish for. You may get it."*** Often when our wishes come true, they don't look or feel quite like we expected.

This may sound strange and many are surprised to find discomfort in living their dream. Why? Well, why not? You may have desired it but you have no idea how it would feel. It's no different than a pair of shoes or a new car that you have been lusting after for a long time. It's new – and it's not comfortable until it gets broken in.

Take a moment to remember what you set out to accomplish. If you have, then relax a bit and enjoy it. You deserve it.

We all recognize that change of any kind generates stress. Even good, wonderful situations such as marriage, a new baby, a new house, a new promotion, a new city, wealth and living your dream. We need to learn and allow ourselves to take the time to "be with it," try it out slowly, sense it, and enjoy it. Become familiar with it. Observe it and give it a chance to feel good. It doesn't really matter what it is. It matters only that we live it completely, with calm, ease and awareness. Remember, we are recovering from a life of "automatic living". It takes effort and time to change that habit.

Don't overreact and go running back to the start line at the first sign of uneasiness. That could be a devastating mistake. Do you recall how you felt on your first day of school in a new class? You managed to get over that.

Despite the vast ocean of good and beautiful things we are blessed with in this world, many find themselves living in small ponds of their own misery. It is familiar, so even if somebody wants to pull them out, they struggle. They don't want to be pulled out of their own misery, or their suffering.

I don't think God meant for us to struggle so much. It's not natural. Have you ever seen a tree depressed? Have you seen a bird anxiety-ridden? Life is not like that at all. Only man (woman) has gone wrong somewhere; we think ourselves to be wiser than nature, than life. A little foolishness and a little wisdom are good. Strive for the right combination.

Here's an inspiring verse to keep by your side in case you start to waiver. Its author is unknown to me.

When things go wrong, as they sometimes will,
When the road you're trudging seems all uphill.
When the funds are low and the debts are high,
And you want to smile, but you have to sigh,
When care is pressing you down a bit –
Rest if you must, but don't you quit.

Life is queer with its twists and turns,
As every one of us sometimes learns,
And many a fellow turns about
When he might have won, had he stuck it out.

Don't give up, though the pace seems slow,
You may succeed with another blow.
Often the goal is nearer than
It seems to a faint and faltering man;
Often the struggler has given up
When he might have captured the victor's cup;
And he learned too late, when the night came down,
How close he was to the golden crown.

Success is failure, turned inside out
The silver tint of the clouds of doubt
And you never can tell, how close you are,
It may be near, when it seems afar;
So stick to the fight when you're hardest hit,
It's when things seem worst, that you mustn't quit.

So whatever new life your dream has enfolded, tweak it; refine it, wear it so it fits. And if, at some time in the future, it no longer feels right, perhaps it will be time to move on to the next dream, the next discovery, the next phase of your life. Nothing in life is permanent. The only constant is change.

Charles Darwin is quoted as saying, ***"It is not necessarily the strongest of the species that survives, nor the most intelligent. It is the most adaptable to change."***

When we look at life as an adventure and are curious about what the journey has in store for us next, we will always find wonderment, rather than worry. Welcome it. See where it leads.

That's the thrill of it all. And perhaps that is the true and only reason for our existence, discovery and personal improvement.

A quote from a passage written by Sarah Ban Breathnach, author of "Simple Abundance" and "Something More."

"Even miracles can be bittersweet but living without them is too dreary to contemplate. Self-created miracles have a way of accumulating until you wake up one morning with a life so rich, you think you're the luckiest person on earth."

Your new life may be the result of the miracle you created, but it does not quite look or feel the way you expected. Is it better than where you were? Can you adapt? Can you make it work? And if the answer were no, don't get discouraged. Figure out how to refine and tweak it. After all, life is a journey – not a destination.

When you reach a higher sense of self awareness or enlightenment and have learned how to be peaceful, you don't just get it once and, live happily ever after. You must continuously work at it, practice, over and over again, in order to maintain that accomplishment. Like any good marriage, it takes constant attention and consciousness. Is it worth the effort? I think so. Don't you?

10

Share your success with others.

One of my beliefs in life, relative to reciprocity is: If you do a favor for someone, they do not owe you. They do not have to return the favor. His or her obligation is to extend the same consideration to someone else, someone in need.

Once you achieve success, share your success with others. Let them enjoy what you have achieved and how you have achieved it. Now, be careful. Let's draw a line between boasting about what you have achieved to express power over others, and, sharing your approach and encouragement as an example for others.

Take the time to give back to others, to your community, however you chose to define it. If you feel that life has been good to you, help others experience it, too. That doesn't mean that you are to start preaching on a soapbox and expect everyone else to live the same life you do. Be willing to help; be available. Let them come to you; don't force yourself on others.

Perhaps, you will choose to mentor others. Or you may choose to work with youth and help influence their life choices. If your new life has given you more free time, perhaps there is that lonely elderly neighbor who could benefit from your youthful energy and wisdom. Select something that fits for you. In the end, you may benefit even more than the recipient of your attention.

In my grandparents' generation, it was important for them to leave an inheritance, often at their expense, no matter how big the sacrifice.

In this twenty-first century, let us focus on leaving a legacy:

- A lesson taught
- A life well lived
- A role model
- A contribution of attitude, of relationships, of faith, of courage.

Make a difference.

Leave a legacy.

And you'll discover that your life does indeed have a purpose.

In closing,

I hope this book has generated some ideas, stimulated your thinking, or mobilized you into action. Or, at least, I hope it has a positive impact by causing you to reflect and get your life in perspective.

Remember it is a journey.
Just as in any marriage, you must work at it every day in order to find some measure of success. It rarely just happens.

So pick it up again. Go back to those chapters that captured your attention, where you may want to spend more time.

Perhaps, five years from now, you'll pick it up again and find something new, something you did not notice before.

And if it brought you pleasure, consider giving it as a gift to someone who might benefit.

And if there is any one point that you would like to explore in greater depth, you may write me through Altern Publications, P.O. Box 206, Waterford, CT 06385 or e-mail me directly at LarsonAMA@aol.com

Margot Larson

round tuit

About the Author

Margot Larson enjoyed many years and a successful career in the Corporate World. When an opportunity presented itself, she set off to start her own business, Management Alternative, LLC, as a consultant currently helping businesses in human resource related matters and coaching entrepreneurs about sound business practices.

Once she stepped away from that corporate scene, she realized that she had been enslaved by it. Work dominated her life. She had postponed trips, worked while on vacation, missed family reunions and, too often, realized that friends seemed to plan events around her business schedule. Looking back with her newfound awareness, she recognized that there was more to life than what others expected of you. She began to examine her priorities, gain clarity and began to build her work around the lifestyle that suited her.

Today, she has a successful business and a small office that suits her needs. She influenced her husband to adopt a better lifestyle, away from the career he disliked. They reduced their debt, liquidated their assets, simplified their lives, and live in a small home (without mortgage) overlooking Long Island Sound. They resisted the need to live up to their earnings, and opted instead to reduce their burdens so that their lifestyle did not require high earnings. In essence they downsized and uncomplicated their lives.

Margot spends a lot of her time coaching and mentoring others who have a desire to make a lifestyle or career change and need help getting there.

In publishing this book, she hopes to provide the inspiration, encouragement and guidance for others to enjoy the same sort of success she has achieved.

Quick Order Form

Fax orders: (860) 691-1580. **Send this form.**
E-mail orders: jumpstartlife@aol.com
Postal Orders: Altern Publications
PO Box 206, Waterford, CT. 06385

Please send me ______ copy(s) of ***"Jump Start Your Life"***

Name: ______________________________

Address: ____________________________

City: _______________________________

State ________________________ Zip Code _____________

Telephone: __________________________

E-mail: _____________________________

Book Cost: US **$10.95**
Canada $14.00

Sales Tax: Please add 6% for books shipped to CT.

Shipping: US **$3.00** per book
Canada $4.00 per book

Payment: Make checks payable to **Altern Publications**

Amount Enclosed: ***$***____________________

Credit Card: Visa MasterCard
Card # ______________________________
Exp. Date: ____/_____

Name on Card: ______________________________________

Quick Order Form

Fax orders: (860) 691-1580. **Send this form.**
E-mail orders: jumpstartlife@aol.com
Postal Orders: Altern Publications
PO Box 206, Waterford, CT. 06385

Please send me ______ copy(s) of ***"Jump Start Your Life"***

Name: ______________________________

Address: ____________________________

City: _______________________________

State ________________________ Zip Code ____________

Telephone: __________________________

E-mail: _____________________________

Book Cost: US **$10.95**
Canada $14.00

Sales Tax: Please add 6% for books shipped to CT.

Shipping: US **$3.00** per book
Canada $4.00 per book

Payment: Make checks payable to **Altern Publications**

Amount Enclosed: ***$***____________________

Credit Card: Visa MasterCard
Card # ______________________________
Exp. Date: ____/_____

Name on Card: ____________________________________